TOUCHED
BY
HIS
SPIRIT

Turning on the flow of the Holy Spirit in *your* life.

JIM HESTERLY

HORIZON**PRESS** / San Diego, CA

Published in San Diego, California by Horizon Press, P.O. Box 17480, San Diego, California 92177.

Library of Congress Cataloging-in-Publication Data available upon request.

Printed in the United States of America

ISBN-13/EAN: 978-1-60412-000-4

This book is dedicated to all those who stood with me and supported this Ministry and especially to my wife June and children James and Robin and many others who have put up with my mistakes and blunders while the Holy Spirit has been teaching me concerning His spiritual gifts.

CONTENTS

FOREWORD

Personally; I love to read books by authors who have experienced their subject matter firsthand. Jim Hesterly, in my estimation, is one of those writers. The Holy Spirit has had theologians and pastors from many different denominations thinking He is something to debate one another over. In reality, the Holy Spirit isn't something to squabble over, but Someone to embrace.

Jesus Christ said that He is the Truth, and later states that the Holy Spirit is the Spirit of truth. As you read this book, let your prayer simply be, "come Holy Spirit—fill me overflowing with the truth of God's love." As the Holy Spirit reveals Jesus to you in new and refreshing ways, absorb the truth and share the truth with others.

In a world that prints daily headlines of death and destruction, we all need some comfort. This book will help you receive the comfort that God's Spirit can bring into your life. Jesus said, "when the Comforter comes." Jesus himself looked at the ministry of the Holy Spirit as that of comfort.

Jim Hesterly has carefully compiled real life insights to help the reader grow and know. He wants this book to help you grow in your understanding of and intimacy with the Person known as the Holy Spirit. And, he wants you to know the Holy Spirit in your daily life.

Many years ago, Jim Hesterly and I became friends—it's not only as a friend that I write this forward; but also as a minister. As a friend I can vouch for Jim's Godly character and his zeal for the things of God's kingdom. As a minister I can endorse Jim's experience and personal relation with the Holy Spirit. This is a refreshing book for the person wanting more of God. May you read it with standing on tip-toe expectation.

Mike MacIntosh
Pastor, Horizon Christian Fellowship
San Diego, California

THE KEY SCRIPTURES

1 Corinthians 12–14

CHAPTER 12

Now concerning spiritual gifts, brethren, I do not want you to be ignorant: You know that you were Gentiles, carried away to these dumb idols, however you were led. Therefore I make known to you that no one speaking by the Spirit of God calls Jesus accursed, and no one can say that Jesus is Lord except by the Holy Spirit.

There are diversities of gifts, but the same Spirit. There are differences of ministries, but the same Lord. And there are diversities of activities, but it is the same God who works all in all. But the manifestation of the Spirit is given to each one for the profit of all: for to one is given the word of wisdom through the Spirit, to another the word of knowledge through the same Spirit, to another faith by the same Spirit, to another gifts of healings by the same Spirit, to another the working of miracles, to another prophecy, to another discerning of spirits, to another different kinds of tongues, to another the interpretation of tongues. But one and the same Spirit works all these things, distributing to each one individually as He wills.

For as the body is one and has many members, but all the members of that one body, being many, are one body, so also is Christ. For by one Spirit we were all baptized into one body—whether Jews or Greeks, whether slaves or free—and have all been made to drink into one Spirit. For in fact the body is not one member but many.

If the foot should say, "Because I am not a hand, I am not of the body," is it therefore not of the body? And if the ear should say, "Because I am not an eye, I am not of the body," is it therefore not of the body? If the whole body were an eye, where would be the hearing? If the whole were hearing, where would be the smelling? But now God has set the members, each one of them, in the body just as He pleased. And if they were all one member, where would the body be?

But now indeed there are many members, yet one body. And the eye cannot say to the hand, "I have no need of you"; nor again the head to the feet, "I have no need of you." No, much rather, those members of the body which seem to be weaker are necessary. And those members of the body which we think to be less honorable, on these we bestow greater honor; and our unpresentable parts have greater modesty, but our presentable parts have no need. But God composed the body, having given greater honor to that part which lacks it, that there should be no schism in the body, but that the members should have the same care for one another. And if one member suffers, all the members suffer with it; or if one member is honored, all the members rejoice with it.

Now you are the body of Christ, and members individually. And God has appointed these in the church: first apostles, second prophets, third teachers, after that miracles, then gifts of healings, helps, administrations, varieties of tongues. Are all apostles? Are all prophets? Are all teachers? Are all workers of miracles? Do all have gifts of healings? Do all speak with tongues? Do all interpret? But earnestly desire the best gifts. And yet I show you a more excellent way.

CHAPTER 13

Though I speak with the tongues of men and of angels, but have not love, I have become sounding brass or a clanging cymbal. And though I have the gift of prophecy, and understand all mysteries and all knowledge, and though I have all faith, so that I could remove mountains, but have not love, I am nothing. And though I bestow all my goods to feed the poor, and though I give my body to be burned, but have not love, it profits me nothing.

Love suffers long and is kind; love does not envy; love does not parade itself, is not puffed up; does not behave rudely, does not seek its own, is not provoked, thinks no evil; does not rejoice in iniquity, but rejoices in the truth; bears all things, believes all things, hopes all things, endures all things.

Love never fails. But whether there are prophecies, they will fail; whether there are tongues, they will cease; whether there is knowledge, it will vanish away. For we know in part and we prophesy in part. But when that which is perfect has come, then that which is in part will be done away.

When I was a child, I spoke as a child, I understood as a child, I thought as a child; but when I became a man, I put away childish things. For now we see in a mirror, dimly, but then face to face. Now I know in part, but then I shall know just as I also am known.

And now abide faith, hope, love, these three; but the greatest of these is love.

Pursue love, and desire spiritual gifts, but especially that you may prophesy. For he who speaks in a tongue does not speak to men but to God, for no one understands him; however, in the spirit he speaks mysteries. But he who prophesies speaks edification and exhortation and comfort to men. He who speaks in a tongue edifies himself, but he who prophesies edifies the church. I wish you all spoke with tongues, but even more that you prophesied; for he who prophesies is greater than he who speaks with tongues, unless indeed he interprets, that the church may receive edification.

But now, brethren, if I come to you speaking with tongues, what shall I profit you unless I speak to you either by revelation, by knowledge, by prophesying, or by teaching? Even things without life, whether flute or harp, when they make a sound, unless they make a distinction in the sounds, how will it be known what is piped or played? For if the trumpet makes an uncertain sound, who will prepare for battle? So likewise you, unless you utter by the tongue words easy to understand, how will it be known what is spoken? For you will be speaking into the air. There are, it may be, so many kinds of languages in the world, and none of them is without significance. Therefore, if I do not know the meaning of the language,

I shall be a foreigner to him who speaks, and he who speaks will be a foreigner to me. Even so you, since you are zealous for spiritual gifts, let it be for the edification of the church that you seek to excel.

Therefore let him who speaks in a tongue pray that he may interpret. For if I pray in a tongue, my spirit prays, but my understanding is unfruitful. What is the conclusion then? I will pray with the spirit, and I will also pray with the understanding. I will sing with the spirit, and I will also sing with the understanding. Otherwise, if you bless with the spirit, how will he who occupies the place of the uninformed say "Amen" at your giving of thanks, since he does not understand what you say? For you indeed give thanks well, but the other is not edified.

I thank my God I speak with tongues more than you all; yet in the church I would rather speak five words with my understanding, that I may teach others also, than ten thousand words in a tongue.

Brethren, do not be children in understanding; however, in malice be babes, but in understanding be mature.

In the law it is written:

"With men of other tongues and other lips I will speak to this people; And yet, for all that, they will not hear Me," says the Lord.

Therefore tongues are for a sign, not to those who believe but to unbelievers; but prophesying is not for unbelievers but for those who believe. Therefore if the whole church comes together in one place, and all speak with tongues, and there come in those who are uninformed or unbelievers, will they not say that you are out of your mind? But if all prophesy, and an unbeliever or an uninformed person comes in, he is convinced by all, he is convicted by all. And thus the secrets of his heart are revealed; and so, falling down on his face, he will worship God and report that God is truly among you.

How is it then, brethren? Whenever you come together, each of you has a psalm, has a teaching, has a tongue, has a revelation, has an interpretation. Let all things be done for edification. If anyone speaks in a tongue, let there be two or at the most three, each in turn, and let one interpret. But if there is no interpreter, let him keep silent in church, and let him speak to himself and to God. Let two or three prophets speak, and let the others judge. But if anything is revealed to another who sits by, let the first keep silent. For you can all prophesy one by one, that all may learn and all may be encouraged. And the spirits of the prophets are subject to the prophets. For God is not the author of confusion but of peace, as in all the churches of the saints.

Let your women keep silent in the churches, for they are not permitted to speak; but they are to be submissive, as the law also says. And if they want to learn something, let them ask their own husbands at home; for it is shameful for women to speak in church.

Or did the word of God come originally from you? Or was it you only that it reached? If anyone thinks himself to be a prophet or spiritual, let him acknowledge that the things which I write to you are the commandments of the Lord. But if anyone is ignorant, let him be ignorant.

Therefore, brethren, desire earnestly to prophesy, and do not forbid to speak with tongues. Let all things be done decently and in order.

INTRODUCTION

The box loomed above all of the other gift bags and wrapped trinkets. The little boy couldn't help sneaking into the living room just to look at it. It was too large to pick up and shake, and taped too tightly to pry a look —but there was no mistaking the name on the tag. It was his. He would open the biggest present on Christmas morning.

Minutes seemed like hours, hours like days, and days like years. The glistening paper and bow tested every ounce of his patience.

When Dad slid the box around the tree and said, "Go ahead," the boy decided to open it slowly. Three seconds later, with wrapping paper still falling to the floor from the height it was thrown, he looked inside. He didn't know what it was. He'd never seen anything like it before. He didn't know how to use it. He didn't really want it. Most of all, he was angry that he didn't get what he wanted.

We sometimes feel these same emotions, ask these same questions, and groan at the same frustrations when we come to faith in Jesus Christ and begin to experience the gifts of the Holy Spirit—because we don't know what they are, we've not seen anything like them before, and we don't know how to exercise them. Throughout my study and teaching on the gifts of the Holy Spirit, I have learned a key principle: If you can understand what the gifts are, you can move from *fear* to *effectiveness*.

This book is divided into three sections. In the first section, I will help you understand what the gifts are, point you to Biblical examples of each gift, show you a contemporary example of the gift in action, and help you understand how the Holy Spirit works through the gift to build His Church. In the second section, I will outline those things we allow in our lives that hinder us from using the gifts. And in the final section, I provide four attitudes we must adopt to discover our gifts. I have also added an Appendix that lists and defines the gifts of the Spirit, along with the appropriate Scripture references.

It is my prayer that we all can grow in our understanding of the Holy Spirit so that we can be more effective in sharing the hope of Christ.

DEFINING THE SPIRITUAL GIFTS

section one

Paul's teaching on the Holy Spirit in 1 Corinthians 12–14 is, perhaps, one of the most misunderstood and misinterpreted passages of Scripture in the New Testament. Many times pastors and teachers will avoid these chapters because even they do not understand nor apply the teaching to their lives. Paul wrote the Corinthian church concerning the gifts of the Holy Spirit because he did not want them to lack any gift or teaching (1 Corinthians 1:7).

Paul knew these mysterious gifts were, and are, essential to the life of a believer and to the church as a whole. These gifts help individuals and churches become (and remain) healthy, vital, and growing. They make up part of the arsenal of spiritual weapons we need today in our fight against principalities, powers, and rulers of darkness in this world.

The gifts must be exercised decently and in order (see 1 Corinthians 14:26-40). When the gifts are exercised properly, unbelievers see evidence that "God is truly among you" (1 Corinthians 14:25).

The gifts of the Spirit are manifestations of His power. When we use the gifts we've been given, truth abounds, many who are sick become well, and God's presence is made manifest to everyone around.

The gifts are not limited to only those who are older in years, those who are mature in the Lord, or those who are educated. The gifts are available to all who are receptive to the work of the Holy Spirit. Several years ago a revival began among the young students at Maranatha Christian Academy, the K-12 private school associated with Calvary Chapel of Costa Mesa. The children began laying their hands upon others and praying for the sick, and many were healed. One woman shared how her five-year-old daughter began to pray in her prayer language, having received the gift of tongues.

God often speaks to us through the gifts of the Spirit when we are gathered together as the body of Christ. We should anticipate and expect it just as the early church experienced it.

In 1 Corinthians 12:4-6, Paul writes, "There are diversities of gifts, but the same Spirit. There are differences of ministries but the same Lord. And there are diversities of activities, but it is the same God who works all in all." There are diverse ways that He will manifest the gifts and diverse ways that He will work through the same gift.

Let me illustrate some of these diversities using two examples of teaching. One teacher serves on Sunday mornings teaching children. Another serves on Wednesday nights instructing adults. The children's teacher hands every child paper and crayons, instructing them to draw pictures of boats and animals while he teaches on the great flood. The teacher of adults uses the method of lecturing to teach the very same passages. The children's teacher would never consider lecturing his students and neither would the adult's teacher consider giving crayons to his students.

Both are teaching, but with different methods. The way one believer exercises the gifts might differ greatly from the way another believer exercises the same gift. For this reason we must be careful not to compare our gift with that of others.

Paul writes that we become fools when we judge ourselves among ourselves and compare ourselves with others. Comparison is the thief of joy. Comparing your gifts and experiences to another can cause you to become prideful or discouraged. Seek the Lord and be faithful to use your gifts despite those around you. God is orchestrating the use of your gifts for His glory. "The manifestation of the Spirit is given to each one for the profit of all" (1 Corinthians 12:7).

In 1 Corinthians 12:8-10, Paul names each of the nine gifts.

- the word of wisdom

- the word of knowledge

- faith

- gifts of healings

- the working of miracles

- prophecy

- discerning of spirits

- tongues

- the interpretation of tongues

Paul is clear: it is the same Spirit who works all of these, distributing to each one individually as He wills. These are all supernatural workings or manifestations of the Spirit. Let us unwrap some of the mystery and seek to understand the gifts and their place in our lives.

THE WORD OF WISDOM

WHAT IS IT?

There are three kinds of wisdom:

- Natural Wisdom: common sense

- Biblical Wisdom: Applying the Bible to your life

- Word of Wisdom: The Holy Spirit speaking God's answer to you; God's solution to a dilemma or problem; God's guidance or direction

EXAMPLES IN SCRIPTURE

Words given in times of need. 2 Kings 4:1-7. In this passage, we see that Elisha was given a word of wisdom by the Lord to help a poor widow. God miraculously provided for the widow to pay her debts, plus a whole lot more. She was faithful to heed Elisha's words.

Words to bring about a peaceful resolution.
Acts 15:1-29. In a caustic situation, God used Paul, Barnabas, Peter, and James to speak the truth in love.

Words to give victory over spiritual warfare.

Joshua 6:1-27. This is the great story of Israel's victory at Jericho. Joshua listened to the Lord and had the people of Israel march around the city. They marched once around the city for six straight days. On the seventh day, they were instructed to march around the city seven times, blowing trumpets and ram's horns. God's words were fulfilled, and the city was destroyed, just as He said. Joshua listened to the voice of the Lord, and victory followed.

Words that tell us about things to come.

Acts 8:26-40. Here we see that Phillip heeded the words of the angel of the Lord to preach the Gospel in the desert to an Ethiopian man. He also listened to the Holy Spirit directing him to the Ethiopian's chariot. Phillip preached the Gospel to the man, and he was baptized. There are so many lessons learned from this powerful story, so take a few moments to read this account in Acts.

EXAMPLES IN EVERYDAY LIFE

Holy Spirit Calling

One day, my wife had the thought to phone an old friend we had not seen for several years. Not knowing for sure that it was the Holy Spirit speaking to her, she kept postponing her call. The feelings of needing to call her continued, so she finally dialed the number. Her friend answered the phone and realizing who was calling, began to weep.

She said, "I am so glad you called today. I have been so discouraged and was just talking with God about what's going on in my life. I told Him that if He didn't do something about it I would end my life."

God knew her situation and put it on my wife's heart to intervene with a phone call. Several years later I saw this friend's husband in the foyer of the church and asked how they were doing.

He said, "We are both doing just great; in fact she's here with me today." God had intervened in her life and kept her from suicide that day by giving a word of wisdom to my wife. The results of edifying others are pretty obvious in this circumstance. If my wife had not listened *and obeyed* God's voice, this lady very well may have killed herself. This was a spiritual battle that was won because the Spirit gave supernatural wisdom.

God is our Realtor

Several years ago, my wife and I moved to San Diego, California. We purchased a condominium, but after nine months the Holy Spirit put it on my heart that we needed to sell it. My wife and I prayed about and discussed all the options and decided to list the condo. Within a few weeks, we sold the property and were pleased with the results. Three months later, the real estate market collapsed. Similar properties earned much less and stayed on the market much longer.

We were thankful to the Lord for His word of wisdom. His wisdom gave us timely direction. The proceeds from the sale supplemented our income while we planted a church in San Diego.

We later saw God's hand in our real estate dealings again. After renting a home for eight years, we felt the Holy Spirit leading us to purchase instead of continuing to rent. My wife felt impressed by the Holy Spirit to withdraw all of our investments in mutual funds and use the resources for the down payment. Our investment counselor told us that we were nuts and financially foolish.

The stock market fell not long after we moved into our new home. Technology stocks and the "dot com" boom were over. Yet, we were financially safe because of the Lord's direction.

HOW DOES THE WORD OF WISDOM EDIFY YOU OR OTHER BELIEVERS?

- Directs us to the solution of a problem or difficulty

- Leads us into the will of God

- Brings guidance to situations or dilemmas in people's lives

WORD OF KNOWLEDGE

WHAT IS IT?

- Supernatural revelation of information we could not know naturally

- Knowledge concerning specific situations, events, or persons

- Information or facts about someone, an event, or an incident in which you had no prior knowledge

EXAMPLES IN SCRIPTURE

In the account of the woman at the well, Jesus knew that the Samarian woman had been married five times. Read this account in John 4:1-26.

Samuel the prophet gathered the nation of Israel together so that God could raise up a king. Through His process, God raised up Saul. When it was time to appoint Saul, they didn't know where he was. The Lord revealed his hiding place to the people—Saul was covered up by the baggage. Take the time to read this insightful story in 1 Samuel 10:17-24.

EXAMPLES IN EVERYDAY LIFE

Henry's Flight

Medical doctor and pastor, Henry Gainey, moved his family to Georgia where he planted a church. Henry's wife, Gale, mentioned that God had spoken to her about a friend, named Jeremy. He was going to die from a serious illness. She encouraged Henry to fly to California and share the Gospel message one more time, giving him another opportunity to receive Christ as his Savior.

Henry landed in California and discovered that Jeremy was in the hospital, and Henry was able to share Christ. This time, Jeremy received Christ as Savior. When Henry returned home, Jeremy was doing fine, but died a few days later from a heart attack. Gale's obedience to the prompting of the Holy Spirit, and Dr. Gainey's obedience to also listen to the Spirit's voice through his wife, led to the salvation of the young man before his death.

Strengthening the Resistance

When Germany invaded Holland during World War II, the Dutch Resistance helped thousands of citizens hide or escape from the Third Reich. Corrie ten Boom, her father, her brother, and her sister played important roles. The Holy Spirit led their efforts minute by minute. The deeper the ten Booms involved themselves and their little watch shop in Haarlem, the more they depended on Him. They had to find sources for food ration cards, transportation, clothing, carpentry, and more. Corrie's brother encouraged her to develop her own sources for their needs. Corrie's story continues:

> "Develop your own sources," Willem had said. And from the moment Fred Koornstra's name had popped into my mind, an uncanny realization had been growing in me. We were friends with half of Haarlem! We knew nurses in the maternity hospital. We knew clerks in the Records office. We knew someone in every business and service in the city.
>
> We didn't know, of course, the political views of all these people. But—and here I felt a strange leap in my heart—God did! My job was simply to follow His leading one step at a time, holding every decision up to Him in prayer. He knew I was not clever or subtle or sophisticated; if the Beje was becoming

a meeting place for need and supply, it was through some strategy far higher than mine.

Within a few days, the Resistance needed help for a Jew they were smuggling. A police officer came to mind. Corrie felt this officer, Rolf, could help. So she prayed.

> That night we held a meeting about Rolf: Betsie and I and the dozen or so teenage boys and girls who acted as messengers for this work. If Rolf had risked his own safety to tell us about Harry's transport, perhaps he should work with us.

> "Lord Jesus," I said aloud, "this could be a danger for all of us and for Rolf, too." But even with the words came a flood of assurance about this man. How long, I wondered, would we be led by this Gift of Knowledge.

They were led for many months as they smuggled Jews, building a safe room in their house, and providing safe transport for the citizens of Haarlem. The Holy Spirit continued to lead them after their capture and during their sentence in Germany's worst concentration and extermination camps. Many Jews, political prisoners, and others came to faith in Christ through their ministry, even in the camps.

HOW DOES THE WORD OF KNOWLEDGE EDIFY YOU OR OTHER BELIEVERS?

- Gives us information that is unknown to us

- Informs us to know how to pray for others

- Provides the catalyst to activate faith to be healed

FAITH

WHAT IS IT?

There are three ways faith is described in the Bible:

Faith is an inward certainty, confidence or trust

Faith is necessary to receive salvation (Ephesians 2:8)

Faith is demonstrated by growing believers; it is the spiritual fruit of a Christian's life (Galatians 5:22-23; Romans 10:17)

Therefore, the spiritual gift of faith is the immediate situation when the Holy Spirit directs a believer to say or do something for a special season, a special moment, or a special need.

EXAMPLES IN SCRIPTURE

- Elijah declared that there would be no rain (1 Kings 17:1-7)

- Peter walked on water (Matthew 14:22-33)

- Mountain-moving faith (Matthew 17:20)

- Peter and John brought healing to a man who was lame from birth (Acts 3:1-16)

- Stephen, full of faith and power, performed great wonders and signs among the people (Acts 6:8)

EXAMPLES IN EVERYDAY LIFE

Daily Milk and Bread

George Mueller cared for orphans in England during the rough days of the mid-19th century. He is remembered for his great faith in God's daily provision. He wrote in his journal that he never tired of "this precious way of depending on the Lord day by day."

Two stories demonstrate the gift of faith in Mueller's life. One evening, all of the children and staff had sat down for dinner, but there was no food. Mueller prayed and gave thanks to God for the food He was about to provide. There was a knock at the door. A milk delivery man stood in the street with his broken wagon behind him, and rather than let the milk spoil, he gave the milk to the orphans.

On another occasion, a baker who had baked too much bread delivered his excess supply to the children. George and the children rejoiced together in all God had abundantly supplied.

Several years ago, a friend had invited me to travel with him to China. The purpose: to smuggle Bibles. I told my friend that if God wanted me to go, He would have to provide the money. I didn't have enough funds at the time.

A short time later, I taught a Bible study at a retreat for high school girls. Not long after that I received an envelope in the mail with a love offering for me from the girls. As I opened the envelope twenty-one dollar bills fell into my lap. Immediately the Holy Spirit said, "That is your China money." I was going to China. I didn't have the rest of the money yet, but the Lord was providing.

There were other hurdles to this trip. I didn't have a passport, a birth certificate (which is needed to acquire a passport), or my inoculation shots. The friend who invited me said, "It's a little late don't you think?"

A few days later, another friend of mine waved me down in a parking lot. I rolled down my window and we had a brief conversation. When we were done, he handed me a piece of paper and jokingly told me to take my wife out for dinner. The piece of paper was a check for $1,500.

On my way to the passport office, I stopped by the travel agency to pick up my airline tickets. I sat in line at the passport office only to have the clerk deny my application, but before I left, the clerk asked if I had my plane tickets. I pulled them out of my pocket and showed them to her. In a few minutes, I had my passport. I didn't know that in order to acquire a passport in one day it was necessary to have a letter from a business sending you to that country or to have the airline tickets in hand. (The regulations have changed since 9/11).

The Lord led me to China and gave me the gift of faith for this special event. He desired me to trust Him for the impossible, and when I returned from China I realized that my entire expenditures had come to the grand total of $1,521. Exactly what He had provided!

HOW DOES FAITH EDIFY YOU OR OTHER BELIEVERS?

- Accomplishes great things for God beyond our control

- Allows you and others to see the power of God

GIFTS OF HEALING

WHAT IS IT?

Healing is a supernatural ability given by God to restore the health of the sick whether spiritually, mentally, or physically.

EXAMPLES IN SCRIPTURE

God Himself is the ultimate example. "I am Yahweh Rapha, the God who heals" (Exodus 15:26).

In the four Gospels, there are 38 events where Jesus performed miraculous works. These works include:

- Jesus traveling about the country healing many

    Then Jesus went about all the cities and villages, teaching in their synagogues, preaching the gospel of the kingdom, and healing every sickness and every disease among the people.
    —Matthew 9:35

- Jesus healing a blind man

So He took the blind man by the hand and led him out of the town. And when He had spit on his eyes and put His hands on him, He asked him if he saw anything. And he looked up and said, "I see men like trees, walking." Then He put His hands on his eyes again and made him look up. And he was restored and saw everyone clearly. Then He sent him away to his house, saying, "Neither go into the town, nor tell anyone in the town."

—Mark 8:23-26

• Jesus healing a crowd of people

And He came down with them and stood on a level place with a crowd of His disciples and a great multitude of people from all Judea and Jerusalem, and from the seacoast of Tyre and Sidon, who came to hear Him and be healed of their diseases, as well as those who were tormented with unclean spirits. And they were healed. And the whole multitude sought to touch Him, for power went out from Him and healed them all.

—Luke 6:17-19

- Jesus healing a crippled man. Read the healing story in John 5:1-15.

The Book of Acts records Phillip preaching the Good News in Samaria and healing people (Acts 8:4-8).

> *Therefore those who were scattered went everywhere preaching the word. Then Philip went down to the city of Samaria and preached Christ to them. And the multitudes with one accord heeded the things spoken by Philip, hearing and seeing the miracles which he did. For unclean spirits, crying with a loud voice, came out of many who were possessed; and many who were paralyzed and lame were healed. And there was great joy in that city.*
> *—Acts 8:4-8*

EXAMPLES IN EVERYDAY LIFE

Layers of Healing

Susan was a part of a Bible study I was leading. She was very depressed, oppressed, and burdened, suffering from great condemnation.

The Holy Spirit gave me a vision about a woman who was sitting in a chair. In the vision, a man came into the room and began to yell at her, "Come on! We've got to go out and make some money!" He then began to drag her out of the house.

The Lord also provided the interpretation for this vision, telling me that someone who had been involved in prostitution before becoming a believer was under great guilt and condemnation. She wasn't being tempted to return to prostitution, but she was not free from the effects of her former lifestyle. Even though she had been forgiven by God, she was still suffering from the guilt and anguish of her past. The Holy Spirit was going to heal her mind and lift her feelings of guilt.

I shared my vision at Bible study. Susan came to the altar. Several ladies came forward to pray with her. The next day, she came to my office and said, "The Holy Spirit gave you that vision about me. God has begun a work of healing in me."

Every time I saw Susan during the following weeks, I marveled at her progress. She would tell me about how God was continuing to remove layers of guilt and condemnation. The radiance of Jesus shone brighter and brighter through her as the Lord healed her completely.

HOW DO GIFTS OF HEALING EDIFY YOU OR OTHER BELIEVERS?

- Can bring health and vigor to the body, soul, and spirit

- Can be used in conjunction with evangelism (Acts 8)

- Shows God's power and complete control of our lives

THE WORKING OF MIRACLES

WHAT IS IT?

Webster defines a miracle as "an extraordinary event manifesting divine intervention in human affairs." The working of miracles is that supernatural work of the Holy Spirit that is contrary to God's natural laws.

EXAMPLES IN SCRIPTURE

- Israel crossing the Red Sea out of Egypt

Then the Egyptians shall know that I am the Lord, when I have gained honor for Myself over Pharaoh, his chariots, and his horsemen." And the Angel of God, who went before the camp of Israel, moved and went behind them; and the pillar of cloud went from before them and stood behind them. So it came between the camp of the Egyptians and the camp of Israel. Thus it was a cloud and darkness to the one, and it gave light by night to the other, so that the one did not come near the other all that night. Then Moses stretched out his hand over the sea; and the Lord caused the sea to go back by a strong east wind all that night, and made the sea into dry land, and the waters were divided. So the children of Israel went into the midst of the sea on the dry ground, and the waters were a wall to them on their right hand and on their left. And the Egyptians pursued and went after them into the midst of the sea, all Pharaoh's horses, his chariots, and his horsemen.

—Exodus 14:18-23

- The water of Jericho was healed when Elisha added salt

Now Josiah also took away all the shrines of the high places that were in the cities of Samaria, which the kings of Israel had made to provoke the Lord to anger; and he did to them according to all the deeds he had done in Bethel. He executed all the priests of the high places who were there, on the altars, and burned men's bones on them; and he returned to Jerusalem. Then the king commanded all the people, saying, "Keep the Passover to the Lord your God, as it is written in this Book

of the Covenant." Such a Passover surely had
never been held since the days of the judges
who judged Israel, nor in all the days of the
kings of Israel and the kings of Judah. But in
the eighteenth year of King Josiah this Passover
was held before the Lord in Jerusalem.
—2 Kings 23:19-23

- Jesus turns water into wine. Read the full account in John 2:1-10

THE PURPOSES OF WORKING MIRACLES

To show God's greatness. Acts 3:13 says, "The God of Abraham, Isaac, and Jacob, the God of our fathers, glorified His Servant Jesus, whom you delivered up and denied in the presence of Pilate, when he was determined to let *Him* go."

To inspire boldness. Acts 4:29 says, "Now, Lord, look on their threats, and grant to Your servants that with all boldness they may speak Your word."

To point people to Jesus. John 20:30-31 says, "And truly Jesus did many other signs in the presence of His disciples, which are not written in this book; but these are written that you may believe that Jesus is the Christ, the Son of God, and that believing you may have life in His name."

To provide protection for God's people. 1 Corinthians 2:4 says, "For out of much affliction and anguish of heart I wrote to you, with many tears, not that you should be grieved, but that you might know the love which I have so abundantly for you."

EXAMPLES IN EVERYDAY LIFE

One More Piece of Wood

During a recent short-term missions trip to Tijuana, Mexico, a building project was short one piece of lumber. A group of men searched the building site, the surrounding area, and the adjacent buildings hoping to find the wood. They decided to leave that part of the wall unfinished, and they began to pray and thank the Lord for all that He had already accomplished that day.

While they were praying, one of the men received a vision. He saw a four-by-four leaning against a wall. He told the others about it and they decided to search all the rooms again. They found a four-by-four exactly the length they needed leaning against the wall just as he had seen in his vision.

Food for Forty

Several years ago, I invited my brother to dinner. I wanted to share the Gospel with him and talk to him about the difference Jesus Christ could make in his life. I invited the rest of my family to come *after* dinner.

My wife, our two children, my brother, and I sat down to our meal at the same moment the doorbell rang. It was my sister. She and her family had come for dinner and brought a steaming loaf of French bread with melted butter and cheese. We welcomed them in and the doorbell rang again. My entire family had come for dinner.

We didn't have nearly enough food for them all, so I called my wife and children together in the kitchen. I asked them to wait to eat until after everyone went home. I would take them out for burgers later that night.

June and I stood alone in the kitchen and asked God to multiply the food. After everyone left, we realized He had worked a miracle. There were approximately 40 people in our house with only enough food for five, yet everyone had eaten and was full. My wife had prepared a small fruit salad, and there was enough left over for several more days.

HOW DOES THE WORKING OF MIRACLES EDIFY YOU OR OTHER BELIEVERS?

- Brings protection to the individual or the church

- Provides necessary items

- Increases little into much

- Overrides laws of nature

FIVE REASONS WHY WE DON'T SEE AS MANY MIRACLES TODAY

1. **Unbelief.** In His hometown of Nazareth, unbelief was so prevalent, Jesus was only able to heal a few sick people (Mark 6:5).

2. **Self-sufficiency.** "Because you say, 'I am rich, have become wealthy, and have need of nothing'—and do not know that you are wretched, miserable, poor, blind and naked" (Revelation 3:17). The church in John's vision was called lukewarm because they had grown complacent and felt they needed nothing from God.

3. **Defining God ourselves.** We have developed preconceived ideas of how God will work and who He will work through. There once was a

man who was casting out demons in the name of Jesus, but he was not a follower with the disciples. The disciples rebuked him and told Jesus what they had done. Jesus remarked to them, "Do not forbid him, for no one who works a miracle in my name can soon afterward speak evil of Me" (Mark 9:38-40). The disciples couldn't imagine that this man was right since he did not work like they worked. Just because someone is ministering in a way that seems strange to you, don't exclude them from fellowship.

4. **Logic.** We simply explain away the miraculous. After Pentecost, some men accused everyone of being full on new wine or drunk. They didn't understand and tried to blame the miracle on other sources without proof (Acts 2:13).

5. **Fear.** Our fear hinders the flow of the ministry of God's Spirit in our lives. Paul exhorted Timothy and reminded him that God had not given him a spirit of fear, but of power, love, and a sound mind (2 Timothy 1:8). The fear of making a mistake or failing will cause disobedience that hinders the Holy Spirit.

PROPHECY

WHAT IS IT?

- Speaking under the direction of the Holy Spirit; through His inspiration

- Can be demonstrated in two ways:

  1. Words given by the Holy Spirit that foretell future events

  2. Words given by the Holy Spirit that build up, stir up, or cheer up

EXAMPLES IN SCRIPTURE

- Philip's daughters prophesied (Acts 21:9)

- Agabus, a prophet, tells Paul how he will be treated (Acts 21:10-14)

- Do not despise prophesying (1 Thessalonians 5:20)

- A gift to be desired (1 Corinthians 14:1)

EXAMPLES IN EVERYDAY LIFE

Debt Free

One evening, several of us were praying and waiting on the Holy Spirit. We received a prophecy regarding a man in deep debt. He owed a great deal of past taxes. The Lord spoke to us that within a year he would be debt-free. The Lord fulfilled this prophecy and before the year came to an end, the Lord provided a buyer for his business, giving him the opportunity to eradicate his debt.

Shepherd's Call

While attending a home Bible study, a new believer who was only about two-weeks old in the Lord saw a vision— sheep were jumping into a funnel. As they fell out the other end they became men who were wearing shepherd's clothing. The interpretation was that all the men in that study would enter the ministry. This was fulfilled as all of them are now in full-time ministry and are serving today in various parts of the world. (I was one of those men and found it encouraging that God would speak in such a way today.)

Messianic Living

I recall an incident in a home Bible study I attended some years ago. After the study, a prophecy was given which had to do with someone who was Jewish. It was a declaration proclaiming Jesus is the Messiah. Immediately after the prophecy was given, a young man who was attending the study for the first time jumped up from his seat and ran into another room. The worship leader followed. They both came out a few minutes later, and the worship leader introduced her brother saying, "We are Jewish. My brother has now come to the conclusion that Jesus is the Messiah and has confesses Him as Savior." The prophecy pierced that young man's heart by the power of the Holy Spirit and he was brought into the kingdom of God.

HOW DOES PROPHECY EDIFY YOU OR OTHER BELIEVERS?

- Brings a word of comfort to the disheartened and discouraged

- Strengthens the believer

- Stirs to action those who may be lethargic

- Prepares us for a future event

HOW DO WE JUDGE PROPHECY?

- Does it line up with God's Word?

- Does it honor Jesus Christ?

- If it is predictive, we must wait on the Holy Spirit to bring it to pass.

DISCERNING OF SPIRITS

WHAT IS IT?

- Ability to understand, to judge, to see, or to know the spirits behind the spiritual activity or behavior

- Know whether or not the source is from God's Holy Spirit, an evil spirit, or the human spirit

- It is not intuition

EXAMPLES IN SCRIPTURE

- Discernment to know when demonic power is at work in someone causing sickness or illness (Matthew 9:32)

- Discernment to know when someone is demon-possessed (Mark 7:32-35)

- Demon-possessed woman spoke the truth but had wrong motives (Acts 16:16)

- Peter knew Satan had influenced Ananias and Sapphira to lie (Acts 5:3)

- Our enemy is unseen. Ephesians 6:11-13 says, "Put on the whole armor of God, that you may be able to stand against the wiles of the devil. For we do not wrestle against flesh and blood, but against principalities, against powers, against the rulers of the darkness of this age, against spiritual hosts of wickedness in the heavenly places. Therefore take up the whole armor of God, that you may be able to withstand in the evil day, and having done all, to stand."

AN EXAMPLE IN EVERYDAY LIFE

A few years ago, a mother and father brought their young daughter to me for prayer, wanting demons cast out. They thought her deafness was caused by demonic powers. Others had tried to deliver her from demonic power but she was not healed.

Many mistakenly believed she was possessed because she behaved strangely. When her parents brought her to church, she made noises that sounded like squeaks and squawks. If they mentioned the name of Jesus, she made the same noises.

As we began to pray the Holy Spirit spoke to us and said that her deafness was not caused by demons, but was simply a physical ailment. Her strange sounds would always occur when they brought her into the church services. While she sat between her parents, she could feel the vibration of their bodies as they were singing and she wanted to join in—but the only sounds she could make sounded like squeaks and squawks. Because we realized she was simply worshiping the Lord in her own manner, we were able to encourage her to continue.

We must always wait on the Holy Spirit's instruction and be careful to avoid making assessments based on the outward appearance of a situation. We must have definite confirmation.

HOW DOES DISCERNING OF SPIRITS EDIFY YOU OR OTHER BELIEVERS?

- Brings protection against the false teachers and prophets

- Identifies the demonic activity

- Reveals the source of spiritual activities

- Helps us to recognize when someone is saying all the right things but for the wrong reason

TONGUES

WHAT IS IT?

The word "tongues" simply means *languages* (*glossa* in the Greek). Quite possibly this refers to languages or dialects that are known or have ceased to exist but were once spoken somewhere in the world. In 1 Corinthians 13:1 Paul speaks of, "the tongues of men or of angels," implying there may be an angelic language. In 1 Corinthians 14:10 we see that each language had its own significance. On the Day of Pentecost, the disciples began to praise God for His wonderful works in languages that were unknown to them but not to the hearers.

EXAMPLES IN SCRIPTURE

- The 120 disciples on the Day of Pentecost (Acts 2:4)

- Twelve men at Ephesus (Acts 19:6)

- Paul had this gift. He also indicates that many of the Corinthian believers had this gift as well (1 Corinthians 14:18)

HOW THE GIFT OF TONGUES IS TO BE USED

The gift of tongues is for prayer, praise, and intercession (1 Corinthians 14:15-17). In this passage we find that we can pray and sing with the Spirit. Paul continues to say that when we pray with the Spirit we are blessing God and giving thanks as well, knowing that this ability is Spirit-inspired and is always directed toward God.

The gift of tongues is most valuable when we desire to pray according to God's will. There may be times we don't specifically know the will of God regarding a situation or need. When we pray with the Spirit we know we are given the supernatural ability for intercession. This enables us to pray without knowing the facts of an entire situation. It is the Holy Spirit who inspires us to pray and He knows all the facts necessary.

Likewise, the gift assists the cry of one's heart in praise and worship of the Lord. There are times when our own natural language cannot adequately express our love and thankfulness toward God. Praying with the Spirit gives a voice to those deepest expressions of adoration and thanksgiving. When we know we are praising, blessing, and giving thanks well, we feel a wonderful sense of fulfillment and confidence.

The apostle Paul says that speaking in tongues is most valuable for our private devotional life (1 Corinthians 14:2, 14). Paul makes it clear that when we pray in tongues our spirit is praying but our mind (intellect) does not understand what is being said (vs. 14). Paul's restrictions regarding the public use of tongues does not apply to the private use of tongues during one's own devotions. When we are speaking only to God and not to men, others don't need to acknowledge or agree with what we are saying.

Praying in tongues is pleasing to God. My mind does not interfere. I'm not limited by my emotions, feelings, or logic. Paul knew that one who speaks in tongues edifies himself. To be edified means to be built up or strengthened spiritually.

The church at Corinth was abusing the gift of tongues in public worship. Paul wrote to the Church to admonish and correct them. He knew the answer to misuse was not *non-use,* but *right use.* Therefore, he contrasted the gift of tongues and the gift of prophecy, knowing that the one who prophesies speaks edification, exhortation, and comfort to people. He who speaks in tongues speaks to God. He was concerned for the good of the church. That's why he exhorted them to excel in edification. He said that in the church it was preferable to speak with his understanding, in a language easily understood by others, so that he could teach others.

HOW DO TONGUES EDIFY YOU OR OTHER BELIEVERS?

- Edifies the rest of the church body when one is faithful to exercise the gift

- Edifies the individual believer who is using the gift, enabling him to give expression of his praise and worship

INTERPRETATION OF TONGUES

WHAT IS IT?

Communicating the essence of what someone else has expressed in tongues.

EXAMPLES IN SCRIPTURE

- Four simple words on the wall were interpreted in many sentences (Daniel 5:25).

- The interpretation is always directed toward God.

For he who speaks in a tongue does not speak to men but to God, for no one understands him; however, in the spirit he speaks mysteries. But he who prophesies speaks edification and exhortation and comfort to men.
—1 Corinthians 14:2-3

HOW DOES THE INTERPRETATION OF TONGUES EDIFY OTHER BELIEVERS?

God bestows the gift of interpretation of tongues for the sake of the entire assembly. The one who speaks with the gift of tongues in the midst of the congregation is built up by the use of the gift, but others do not understand. When the interpretation is given, all can be edified and understanding can be experienced by all.

HINDERING
THE HOLY SPIRIT

section two

Recently, I heard the following statement: "The greatest hindrance to the flow of God's Spirit in our lives is not others, but ourselves." I find that there are at least six things that hinder the flow the Holy Spirit and His gifts in our lives. In this chapter we will discuss and uncover the six hindrances. Paul asked the Galatian church, "Who hindered you from obeying the truth?" (Galatians 5:7). Perhaps we should ask ourselves the same question: what hinders us from obeying the truth? Paul compared the Christian life to running a race. In the same manner that a runner lays aside every extra weight or care that would slow him down, we should get rid of those things that hinder the work of the Spirit in our lives.

We can only get rid of a hindrance when we can recognize it. I hope that through this discussion, you will recognize the hindrances in your life and use the encouragement and lessons in this chapter to correct and overcome them. You cannot overcome these hindrances by yourself, so I have included a simple prayer of help at the end of each section. Take the time to really pray these prayers and allow the Holy Spirit's help to give you victory over these obstacles to His work in your life.

IGNORANCE

Ignorance can be a huge hindrance to the work of the Spirit in our lives. Paul was so concerned that the believers might remain ignorant concerning the gifts. He wrote to the church in Corinth to set them straight. Ignorance is a lack of knowledge. When Paul wrote that he did not want the believers to be ignorant, he did not mean that they were stupid. The believers were merely untaught, uninformed, inexperienced, unfamiliar, or still in the dark about the gifts of the Spirit.

WHAT THE BIBLE SAYS ABOUT IGNORANCE

Apollos was a good teacher. The Bible says he was "an eloquent man and mighty in the Scriptures" (Acts 18:24). He was, however, limited in some areas of ministry because he was uninformed concerning the work of the Holy Spirit. Aquila and Priscilla took him under their wing to teach and disciple him more fully in "the way of God." Paul arrived in Ephesus and met with the believers and asked some of Apollos' disciples if they had received the Holy Spirit when they believed. They responded, "We have not so much as heard whether there is a Holy Spirit."

They were untaught, uninformed, and unfamiliar with the teaching about the Holy Spirit. Read the full account in Acts, chapters 18 and 19.

A CONTEMPORARY EXAMPLE OF IGNORANCE

The contemporary church struggles with ignorance when it comes to the more vocal gifts of prophecy, tongues, and the interpretation of tongues. We misunderstand Paul's teaching in 1 Corinthians 14.

As we've previously seen, when someone speaks in tongues, they are speaking to God (1 Corinthians 14:2). The interpretation should, therefore, also be directed *toward the Lord*, not other believers. For example, if a prophecy is given immediately after someone speaks out in a tongue, some consider that to be the interpretation, however, this is erroneous. What they consider be the interpretation is actually directed toward the people and not toward God. Therefore, it must be considered a prophecy, rather than the interpretation of tongues. Out of ignorance, someone gives a prophecy because he is so excited that God has given him a word. However, according to Paul's instructions in 1 Corinthians 14 we should wait until an interpretation is given before proceeding. Remember, the interpretation should always be directed toward God.

WHAT CAN I DO TO STOP IGNORING THE GIFTS?

In 1 Corinthians 14:38, Paul says, "If anyone is ignorant, let him be ignorant." We can't force someone to agree with what the Scripture says. All we can do is to instruct them according to the Word of God.

The best antidotes for ignorance are Bible study and solid teaching. There is no excuse for ignorance because we have an abundance of resources available to us— books, audio and video messages on the internet, and many solid Bible-teaching churches. We should be like the Berean Church (Acts 17:11) who received the Word with all readiness, and searched the Scriptures daily.

A PRAYER FOR HELP

Father, I know that my ignorance comes from the lack of teaching and understanding. Please help me study Your Word and take to heart all the lessons regarding the ministry of the Holy Spirit.

NEGLECT

To neglect something means to think under rate or under value. We must never think lightly of the gifts of the Holy Spirit. They are vital to the spiritual health of the body of Christ.

WHAT THE BIBLE SAYS ABOUT NEGLECT

Paul only wrote one letter to correct the abuses of the gifts of the Spirit (1 Corinthians). But in three of his letters, he addressed the Church's neglect of the gifts of the Spirit.

In 1 Timothy 4:14, we read, "Do not neglect the gift that is in you, which was given to you by prophecy with the laying on of the hands of the eldership." We are not told which gift Timothy received. Since we are told it came because of the laying on of hands, one of the elders apparently prophesied to him about it. Somehow, this gift had been put aside and was being neglected. He was not using God's gift. Every gift is necessary and important for the building up and strengthening of the Body of Christ. Scholars believe that Timothy was pastor of the church at Ephesus at the time, so we see that even those in leadership positions in the church can neglect gifts.

In 2 Timothy 1:6, Paul reminds Timothy about his gift, "Therefore I remind you to stir up the gift of God which is in you through the laying on of hands." Apparently he did not heed Paul's earlier exhortation. Paul used a graphic statement—stir up—which means, "to fan into a flame." It is quite possible that Paul was the one of the elders who laid hands on Timothy.

The third time Paul addressed the neglect of the gifts is recorded in 1 Thessalonians 5:20-21, "Do not despise prophecies. Test all things; hold fast what is good." Paul exhorted the church about neglect because they were quenching the Spirit (vs. 19) like water being thrown on a brilliant campfire. Quenching the Spirit occurs when we neglect to exercise His gifts or when we are moving in the realm of our flesh.

Peter also addresses the issue of neglect in his writings. In 1 Peter 4:10, he writes, "As each one has received a gift, minister it to one another, as good stewards of the manifold grace of God." Here we see the relationship between stewardship and the gifts. The Bible is clear that if we neglect our gifts, we are poor stewards.

CONTEMPORARY EXAMPLES OF NEGLECT

Neglect Can Lead to Breakdown

During my high school years, a friend's dad owned a huge earth moving truck. Every Saturday he had the job of crawling underneath the truck and greasing all the fittings. The work was precise. If he missed one of those fittings the truck could break down which would hinder his dad from earning a living. When he finished his work, he put a mark on a checklist signifying his careful completion of the work, showing that he had not neglected any detail. When we neglect a gift that God has given us, it can hinder the work of the Holy Spirit in the Body of Christ, in our neighborhoods, and in our city.

Losing Your Fragrance

Early in my marriage to June, I purchased a bottle of Chanel No. 5 perfume as a gift for a special occasion. At the time, Chanel was one of the most expensive perfumes. I hoped this gift would express my love and affection, but because it was so expensive she only decided to save it only for special occasions. I recently found the bottle of perfume on her counter top. It has a residue of the perfume, but when I opened it I discovered that the perfume had lost its fragrance.

I do not believe that God removes the gifts of the Spirit because in Romans 11:29 we read that the "gifts and the calling of God are irrevocable." This means that God does not take them away from us. I do believe, however, that if we neglect them they lose their power, just as my wife's perfume lost its fragrance and power over the years. In the same way, if we have the gift of tongues and neglect to use it we will discover that it has lost its power in our lives. Paul said that if we speak in tongues we will be edified. If we have the gift of tongues and fail to use that gift we do not receive the benefit of it. This principle can be applied to all of the gifts. If they are neglected in our lives we will become powerless and lose all benefits that could be derived from their exercise.

HOW CAN I STOP NEGLECTING THE GIFTS?

Paul's prescription to Timothy remains the best remedy— stir up your gift. To stir up means to fan as you would a fire that has died down. You can stir up your gift by acknowledging that you have neglected a gift, asking for God's forgiveness, then making yourself available to Him once more.

Gifts are like muscles. If we do not use them they become weak or stiff and inflexible. However, as we begin to use a muscle it becomes strong again. And so it is with the gifts. They once more become strong as we begin to exercise them.

A PRAYER FOR HELP

Lord, I have been like Timothy and neglected the gift You've given me. Please help me stir up the gift. Help me make myself open and available to You. I want to obey Your Holy Spirit.

FEAR

Fear is the opposite of faith. Faith is trusting in God to do what He says He will do. Often it is the unknown that makes us fearful. Not knowing how others will respond to the way a gift is ministered can cause fear. Being fearful or overly concerned about the opinions of other is a great hindrance to the flow of God's Spirit. Sometimes our fear stems from past failures or mistakes, but our fear of failure has its root in pride.

WHAT THE BIBLE SAYS ABOUT FEAR

King Saul feared defeat by the Philistines. He cowered in the city of Gilgal. His own people were leaving, so Saul took matters into his own hands and offered a burnt offering that only priests were qualified to offer. Samuel, the prophet, rebuked Saul because of his disobedience which was caused by fear. Read the full story in 1 Samuel 13:1-15.

When the nation of Israel drew near to the Promised Land, Moses selected twelve spies to enter the Land and return with a report. Ten spies came back with a bad report. They were fearful of the people who lived in the Promised Land. They said, "The land...devours its inhabitants....There we saw giants...we were like grasshoppers in our own sight" (Numbers 13:31-33). They were ignorant concerning God's promise and His power and gave into their fear.

In Matthew 14:22-33, we see that Jesus' disciples also struggled with fear. After Jesus fed the multitude, Jesus sent his disciples to the other side of the Sea of Galilee. Late at night, Jesus walked out to them—on the water. When they saw the shape of man, they cried out, "It's a ghost!"

Jesus spoke to them and calmed them down. Peter asked to join Jesus on the water and for a few seconds, Peter walked on the water. He looked around him, he saw the waves, and began to sink in great fear. He took his eyes off of Jesus and trusted in himself. He lacked faith.

We become afraid because we lack faith in God and do not understand His love. John wrote, "There is no fear in love but perfect love casts out fear, because fear involves torment. But he who fears has not been made perfect in love" (John 4:18).

Fear was also crippling Timothy and caused him to neglect his gift. Paul wrote, "For God has not given us a spirit of fear, but of power and of love and of a sound mind" (2 Timothy 1:7).

CONTEMPORARY EXAMPLES OF FEAR

Was it the Lord?

Learning to hear God's voice is a process. Young believers often fear they are not hearing from the Lord, only their own imaginations. Often, after a time of prayer when we have been waiting on the Holy Spirit, someone will come up to me and say, "I thought perhaps God was giving me a word or a vision, but I was afraid to speak it out. I wasn't sure that it was God speaking."

We are all learning to recognize God's voice as He speaks to us. When this happens, I encourage the fearful one to say, "I have this thought going through my mind. I'm not sure if it is God or not, but please let me share it." Speaking up can be frightening, but all of the gifts of the Spirit are ministered by faith.

Step Out in Faith

I still become fearful from time to time. I remember attending a pastor's conference when many of the pastor's wives also attended. I was leading a time of waiting on the

Holy Spirit called an afterglow. The Holy Spirit gave me a word of knowledge. One of the couples was struggling in a very specific area. The Lord did not identify the couple, but urged me to share the word of knowledge with the group. All of a sudden, fear gripped me. I worried that no one would respond. My pastor was sitting in the front row. What would he think if I spoke a word and no one responded? The Holy Spirit pressed me to speak because He wanted to heal the marriage. I obeyed and spoke the word. My pastor then spoke up and confirmed it, saying that the Lord had also given him the very same thought. The couple's marriage was healed through the work of the Holy Spirit in their lives.

HOW CAN I OVERCOME FEAR?

We overcome fear by keeping ourselves in the love of God. Jude 20-21 says, "But you, beloved, building yourselves up on your most holy faith, praying in the Holy Spirit, keep yourselves in the love of God, looking for the mercy of our Lord Jesus Christ unto eternal life." We are also reminded of God's mercy and love when we read and study the Scriptures. As we immerse ourselves in His love, by searching the Scriptures, God reminds us of His faithfulness in the past to meet our needs and our faith grows for the present and for the future.

God is not an angry God who is just waiting for us to make mistakes. He is a loving and merciful Father in heaven. He understands our weaknesses and He longs to help our fear subside.

Write 2 Timothy 1:7 on a note card and keep it with you. When you become fearful, read this verse and feel the strength of the Lord.

> *"For God has not given us a spirit of fear, but*
> *of power and of love and of a sound mind."*
> *–2 Timothy 1:7*

A PRAYER FOR HELP

Father, I realize that fear does not come from You. The Bible tells me that You have not given me a spirit of fear but of power love and a sound mind. Please help me overcome my fear. I want to receive Your love and power. Help me think clearly about the work of the Spirit in my life.

COMPARISON

The issue of comparison was another of Paul's motivations for writing 1 Corinthians. Comparing your gift with that of another believer can lead to discouragement or pride. Comparison takes our eyes off of Jesus and places them on ourselves. A pastor friend of mine said he doesn't even compare this week's message with last week's message because of pride or discouragement. When we compare, we are tempted to "compete" with others because we want to have the most spectacular gift. Comparison is the thief of joy.

WHAT THE BIBLE SAYS ABOUT COMPARISON

In 2 Corinthians 10:12 Paul wrote, "For we dare not class ourselves or compare ourselves with those who commend themselves. But they, measuring themselves by themselves, and comparing themselves among themselves, are not wise." When we compare our gifts with those of other believers we open ourselves to either pride or discouragement. Pride will invade because we think we are better than others. Discouragement comes when we feel inadequate.

Jesus spoke a parable about the Pharisee who compared his prayer to the tax collector's.

> *"Two men went up to the temple to pray, one a Pharisee and the other a tax collector. The Pharisee stood and prayed thus with himself, 'God, I thank You that I am not like other men—extortioners, unjust, adulterers, or even as this tax collector. I fast twice a week; I give tithes of all that I possess.' And the tax collector, standing afar off, would not so much as raise his eyes to heaven, but beat his breast, saying, 'God, be merciful to me a sinner!' I tell you, this man went down to his house justified rather than the other; for everyone who exalts himself will be humbled, and he who humbles himself will be exalted."*
> *—Luke 18:10-14*

Jesus makes it clear that comparing only brings about a future humbling before God. Jesus was concerned with the heart of the matter—the heart attitude.

In 1 Corinthians 12, Paul shows us the danger of comparison. He uses the analogy of the human body and reminds us that each part of the body is necessary. When we consider the hand and the foot, we see they are similar yet have different functions. The foot is designed to help us walk. Our toes provide balance and stability. The hand has a different purpose. The fingers are good for pointing, scratching, grasping, playing musical instruments, and comforting a child. The foot is used to carry the body to different places, while the hand is used to tie the shoelaces. Each part of the human body has different function, but each is necessary.

CONTEMPORARY EXAMPLES OF COMPARISON

Eric's Dilemma

Eric was a talented musician and led the choir at his church, but he was also supernaturally gifted in one-on-one counseling. He spent most of his time working on the outward gift—music—but was often frustrated. When he realized his gift for counseling, and began to understand and exercise it, his frustrations disappeared. He stopped trying to be and do what God had not gifted him to do—perform. He became fulfilled and joyful as he began to counsel others.

Confidently Using Your Gifts

I was raised in a church that believed the spiritual gifts ended at the time of the apostles. They denied their existence today and didn't teach on them. Therefore, I was not open to the gifts, not even the gift of tongues.

However, as I began to study what the Bible said about the gift of tongues, I realized what I had been missing. It is a good gift from God! Over time, I finally received it. But it didn't take me long to begin comparing the sound of my gift of tongues to others. I regularly compared myself to my wife when she spoke in tongues.

I was discouraged often. Her language was beautiful and sweet, but mine was guttural and coarse. I only had a few sounds, but she had many. Often, I resisted the Holy Spirit's prompting to pray using my gift. When I stopped comparing my gift with hers, I began to experience a thankful heart and freedom in my worship as I began to freely use the gift God had given me.

HOW TO STOP COMPARING

We must accept the fact that each one of us is uniquely created by God. There are no two human beings alike on earth or throughout history. Not even identical twins are exactly the same.

We must recognize that the Holy Spirit gives according to His will. Each believer is gifted according to God's master plan to encourage and edify the church as a whole. Our responsibility is to be thankful for the gifts of God has given us.

Comparing can lead to jealousy and competition. Gifts do not make us more spiritual. Our gifts are simple tools that help us as we minister to and serve others. We did not earn them. We do not deserve them.

A PRAYER FOR HELP

Heavenly Father, I do not want to be envious or jealous of other's gifts. I want to be thankful for those that You've given me. Please help me to have a thankful heart.

INFLEXIBILITY

Inflexible people are stubborn, unyielding, and have hardened their hearts. When we are inflexible we are set in our own ways. Paul reminds us that love does not demand its own way (1 Corinthians 13:5). God's ways are not our ways (Isaiah 55:8, 9). God called the Israelites stiff-necked and stubborn because they always resisted His plans (Exodus 32:9). When we become stubborn or unyielding we become inflexible and unusable to the Holy Spirit.

WHAT THE BIBLE SAYS ABOUT BEING INFLEXIBLE

One day, Jesus suggested that His disciples should launch out into deeper water. He assured them they would catch more fish there. Peter objected because they had fished all night and caught nothing, however he finally followed Jesus' instructions. When they pulled in their nets, they were filled with fish. Peter was being unyielding at the beginning but changed his mind and became flexible. Peter was a fisherman and Jesus was a carpenter. Perhaps Peter was thinking, *Jesus, you are a carpenter. You know how to make furniture. I'm the fisherman and I know how to fish. Don't tell me how to do my job* (Luke 5:4-7).

Much later, after His resurrection, Jesus again asked the disciples if they had any fish. "No," they answered. Jesus told them to cast their net on the right side of the boat and they would catch many. In obedience, they dropped the net on the other side of the boat and caught a full net of fish. They had finally learned the blessing of flexibility.

I believe when we are inflexible we hinder the flow the Holy Spirit. Paul was given a vision. He saw a *man* from Macedonia calling out to him for help. However, the first people they found who were interested in what they had to share were *women*. Lydia invited them to use her home for a Bible study. Paul could have been inflexible and thought to himself, *I was called by a man and so must find the man.*

During His ministry, Jesus was often questioned by the religious leaders. One day, the Pharisees tried to trick Jesus with questions about fasting. Jesus responded, "No one puts new wine into old wineskins; or else the new wine bursts the wineskins, the wine is spilled, and the wineskins are ruined. But new wine must be put into new wineskins" (Mark 2:22). Old wineskins are leather bags that have become stiff and rigid. They are inflexible. Pouring liquid into them would cause them to come apart at the seams. When we become like old wineskins, it becomes difficult for the Holy Spirit to use us.

Gideon had to be flexible. His army was 22,000 soldiers strong, but when the Lord wanted Gideon to go against the Amalekite camp He reduced the force to 300. Gideon trusted God's direction instead of bristling against the direction. Read the full account in Judges 7.

A CONTEMPORARY EXAMPLE OF INFLEXIBILITY

Pastor Kendrick remembers a Sunday morning when he had to be flexible. The normal order of worship at his church was two hymns sung by the choir, announcements, the morning offering, the pastor's teaching, and perhaps an altar call. On that particular Sunday morning, he felt the Holy Spirit prompting him. "Stand up and preach now." The service had barely begun. The congregation was only singing the first hymn. The pastor rejected the idea because he thought he might be out of order and it would disrupt the flow of the morning, but the Holy Spirit kept prodding him. The pastor caught the attention of the choir director and asked him to stop. The pastor then asked a young man from the choir to share his story of being set free from drugs. Pastor Kendrick then gave a very short salvation message and invited those who wanted to accept Jesus' free gift of salvation to come forward to the altar. The front of the church was filled with people receiving Christ as Savior. In that moment the pastor understood why God wanted him to preach right away.

But another blessing awaited. A few days later, a man from another state called the pastor to say thank you, explaining that he and his family had been in town on business. They decided to visit the church even though he only had about 15 minutes to spare before they would need to leave for the airport. He related how his son would not attend church with them when at home but he came into the church with them that Sunday. Their son received Christ as Savior that morning.

Pastor Kendrick realized that if he had been inflexible about the order of service, this young man may not have accepted Christ.

HOW CAN I STOP BEING INFLEXIBLE?

Flexible believers try to be available and faithful with what God has given them. If you only have two words or sounds in tongues, then speak those two words in faith. If God gives you a short prophecy, then speak it out. When God gives you a word of knowledge for someone, go minister it to them. God will use your faithfulness for His purposes. Then He'll begin to increase your gifts and ministry. Faithfulness in the small things can open wonderful opportunities to minister the gifts of the Spirit.

A PRAYER FOR HELP

Lord, I have become inflexible. I don't want to be like an old wineskin anymore. When changes and surprises come, please help me to trust You and follow Your plan.

SIN

Sin grieves the Holy Spirit. If we continually practice sin, the Holy Spirit will be hindered in His work through us. Sin is disobedience and breaks our fellowship with the Lord which causes us to disobey Him and a failure to recognize His voice as He speaks to us. Look at what Paul says in the Book of Ephesians.

> *Let no corrupt word proceed out of your mouth, but what is good for necessary edification, that it may impart grace to the hearers. And do not grieve the Holy Spirit of God, by whom you were sealed for the day of redemption. Let all bitterness, wrath, anger, clamor, and evil speaking be put away from you, with all malice. And be kind to one another, tenderhearted, forgiving one another, even as God in Christ forgave you.*
> *–Ephesians 4:29-32*

Sin also quenches the work of the Holy Spirit in the life of a believer. David, because of his adultery with Bathsheba, prayed that God would not remove the Holy

Spirit from him. Psalm 51 describes David's heartfelt anguish concerning his sin.

WHAT THE BIBLE SAYS ABOUT SIN

Samson allowed fleshly desires—sin—to control his actions. God removed Samson's power and strength. God responded to his repentant heart and Samson's strength was restored. He was then able to pull down the pillars of the building, bringing destruction upon the Philistines (Judges 13, 14).

God does not remove His Holy Spirit from any individual today, as He did in the Old Testament period. However, we see that God says sin will quench the work of the Holy Spirit in a believer's life. Time and time again, power is lost in the life of an individual when sin dominates.

The Holy Spirit brings conviction of our sin. If we resist His convicting and continue in sin, we become hardened to the things that are spiritual and careless with our familiarity to living in the flesh. Our sin closes the door on the Spirit's power.

When we walk in un-confessed sin we give power to the enemy, the devil. He will take advantage of our weakened state. He condemns us. He tempts us more.

His efforts make us feel unworthy and unusable. We delay seeking the forgiveness of our loving and gracious God. If there is a particular sin we practice—a besetting sin we have not confessed, the Spirit's *power* will be removed. However, John reminds us that, "If we confess our sins, He is faithful and just to forgive us our sins and to cleanse us from all unrighteousness" (1 John 1:9).

Achan's story is a powerful example of how disobedience affects the flow of the Spirit. After the landmark victory at Jericho, the Israelites were defeated at Ai. The Lord removed His hand from the army because Achan disobeyed God's direction. He kept some of the spoils of war for himself and hid them under the floor of his tent. He gave in to the temptation of the flesh, and although he kept it hidden from the people, God knew all about it (Joshua 6-8).

CONTEMPORARY EXAMPLES OF SIN

Brooklyn Blues

Jim Cymbala, who is pastor of The Brooklyn Tabernacle in New York City, writes in his book, *Fresh Wind, Fresh Fire,* about a time when the Holy Spirit was moving powerfully. Jim felt strongly that the Spirit was being quenched somewhere in the church. Cymbala didn't know the exact problem, but he prayed and asked God to reveal it in order to bring about repentance and restoration. God convicted an usher of his sin of stealing from the weekly offerings. He came forward in repentance. The Holy Spirit began to move once again through that church.

Busing Problems

Thomas felt led by the Holy Spirit to begin a bus ministry to help children come to church on Sunday mornings. The Holy Spirit moved in his heart to support the project with a $1,000 gift, but when the time came to give the money, he only donated $500, disobeying the Spirit's direction. A few months later, the same church began a building campaign. Members were encouraged to invest at amounts like $100, $250, and $500. The Holy Spirit reminded Thomas that he had already committed to give $1,000 to the bus project, but he purchased a coupon for $250 ignoring the Spirit's prompting once more.

During this time, Thomas' business began to dwindle and subsequently ground to a halt. No revenue came in. He decided if there were any more coupons available for the church building project he would buy one at Wednesday night's service. The pastor informed the church that the goal had almost been met. When Thomas went to purchase his coupon, only one remained. It was for $250.

Amazingly, his business received a large amount of orders the next day. The total equaled an entire month's worth of orders. The Holy Spirit reminded Thomas of his first commitment of $1,000 that he had not fulfilled. He knew that he had disobeyed God. His revenue in the business stopped until he fulfilled his promise. His disobedience was hindering the flow of the Spirit, not only in Thomas' personal life, but in his business. His broken promise affected him personally, but it also affected his wife, his children, his employees, his vendors, and so on. The Apostle Paul writes, "If one part hurts, every other part is involved in the hurt, and in the healing" (1 Corinthians 12:26, MSG). When we are disobedient to God's instructions to us it hurts our own fellowship with Him and hinders the flow of the Spirit in the whole church, the body of Christ.

HOW CAN I STOP SINNING?

When John received his revelation, he saw visions of seven churches. One of those churches lost its "first love." Jesus spoke to this church saying, "Remember therefore from where you have fallen; repent and do the first works" (Revelation 2:5). He gave them three Rs, remember, repent, and return. Let me suggest four Rs as you strive to stop sinning:

- **Remember** how and what God has done for you.

- **Repent** from your sins. Repent means to turn around or make a U-turn. You need to change your direction.

- **Return** and practice the spiritual activities in which you invested before your sin. Go to church, Bible study, meet with friends, pray, read the Bible, etc.

- **Renew** your commitment to serve the Lord. Pray and ask the Lord to guide you in new and fresh ways.

A PRAYER FOR HELP

Thank you, Father, for showing me my sin. I repent of it. Help me to turn away from my sin and move toward You. Please restore the fellowship we had. In Jesus' name, Amen.

DISCOVERING YOUR PERSONAL GIFTS

section three

The apostle Paul encouraged and exhorted the Corinthian church to desire spiritual gifts. We are now the heirs of this message as we read his letter we know as 1 Corinthians. Paul understood the value of these gifts. He experienced several himself.

Many people long for the gifts, but their lack of knowledge about them keeps them from discovering them. I am asked two questions above all others:

"How do I discover my gifts?"

"Can I receive more than one gift?"

In this section you will discover five foundational truths to help you discover your gifts.

BE AVAILABLE

To be available means to put all that you have—your talents, time, abilities, finances, personality traits—at His disposal. To be available means to be handy, ready, convenient and usable. We put ourselves at God's disposal for His purpose and pleasure. The staff of our nation's President is coached to respond to inquiries by saying, "I serve at the pleasure of the President." Do you serve at the pleasure of the King of kings?

Paul expresses this attitude in his letter to the church in Rome. He writes, "present your body a living sacrifice, holy, acceptable to God, which is your reasonable service" (Romans 12:1). Paul coached his protégé, Timothy, to "Preach the word! Be ready in season and out of season. Convince, rebuke, exhort, with all longsuffering and teaching" (2 Timothy 4:2). Practically-speaking, this means we must to be ready to do whatever God wants us to do on His timetable with whatever resources He has or will supply.

Ministry is not always convenient. It was not convenient for Ananias to stop whatever he was doing to go across town.

> *Now there was a certain disciple at Damascus named Ananias; and to him the Lord said in a vision, "Ananias." And he said, "Here I am, Lord."*

> *"So the Lord said to him, "Arise and go to the street called Straight, and inquire at the house of Judas for one called Saul of tarsus, for behold, he is praying.*

> *"And in a vision he has seen a man named Ananias coming in and putting his hand on him, so that he might receive his sight."*
> *—Acts 9:10-12*

Ananias' response should be our response when the Lord moves in our hearts: "Here I am, Lord." And like Ananias, what the Holy Spirit says to us might frighten us.

> *Then Ananias answered, "Lord I have heard from many about this man, how much harm he has done to your saints in Jerusalem.*

"And here he has authority from the chief priests to bind all who call on Your name."
—Acts 9:13-14

What the Lord might ask may be dangerous or uncomfortable, as it was for Ananias, but God already knows this. He is the One Who may be sending you on the mission.

But the Lord said to him, "Go, for he is a chosen vessel of Mine to bear My name before Gentiles, kings, and the children of Israel. For I will show him how many things he must suffer for My name's sake." And Ananias went his way and entered the house.
—Acts 9:15-17a

The most reasonable, sensible, and spiritual thing that we can do is present ourselves to God. When we consider all that He has given to us, the decision should be an easy one.

Yet many times, we act like the ship, *Californian,* on April 15, 1912.

At the time the *Titanic* hit an iceberg in the North Atlantic; a ship by the name of the *Californian* was only ten miles away. Unfortunately, the *Californian* had tuned out and had turned off its ship's radio.

The *Carpathia* was a greater distance away, but its radio was on. This ship heard the distress signal of the Titanic and came to the rescue as quickly as possible, but many lives were lost by the time she arrived. Once she arrived she was able to save hundreds of lives. But it was the *Californian* that could have been instrumental in saving many, many more lives had she only been listening.

Is your spiritual "radio" on? Are you listening? Are you available? Will you respond?

A PRAYER FOR HELP

Dear Father, please help me to tune in, listen to, and respond to Your Word. I want to always be available to do what You ask. Give me a loving heart, a listening ear, and a willing attitude. Thank you for hearing and answering my prayer. Gratefully, I pray in Jesus' name, Amen.

BE HUMBLE

Being humble doesn't mean we consider ourselves worthless, speak ill of our talents, contribute nothing, or sit silently on the sidelines. Being humble means accepting our own gifts and abilities as gifts from God. Being humble means realizing that we are not the most important people around. Life is not all about us. We are not the center of the universe.

Right after Paul exhorted the Roman church to present themselves as living sacrifices, he said, "For I say, through the grace given to me, to everyone who is among you, not to think of himself more highly than he ought to think, but to think soberly, as God has dealt to each one a measure of faith" (Romans 12:3). This type of thinking brings humility, modesty, and an unassuming attitude. We assume the behavior and heart of a servant.

Paul explains this servant attitude in greater detail through his letter to the Philippian church.

> *Do nothing out of selfish ambition or vain conceit, but in humility consider others better than yourselves. Each of you should look*

not only to your own interests, but also to the interests of others. Your attitude should be the same as that of Christ Jesus: Who, being in very nature God, did not consider equality with God something to be grasped, but made himself nothing, taking the very nature of a servant, being made in human likeness. And being found in appearance as a man, he humbled himself and became obedient to death—even death on a cross!
—Philippians 2:3-8, NIV

Humility is the opposite of pride. Perhaps no person in the Scriptures knew this better than Peter. Peter had a wonderful experience of walking on the water (Matthew 14:22-36). Peter brazenly declared Jesus' deity (Matthew 16:13-20). But Peter was also brought low, to a place of humility. Jesus washed Peter's feet (John 13:1-11). Peter sank amid the waves (Matthew 14:22-36). Peter denied Christ around the campfire (Mark 14:66-72). When Peter writes his letters, humility is a key theme. For example, 1 Peter 5:3b-7 says:

Be clothed with humility, for "God resists the proud, But gives grace to the humble." Therefore humble yourselves under the mighty

*hand of God, that He may exalt you in due
time, casting all your care upon Him, for He
cares for you.*

One of Solomon's proverbs packs a punch. "A man's
pride shall bring him low: but honor shall uphold the
humble in spirit." *–Proverbs 29:23, KJV*

Jesus Himself painted one of the most vivid pictures
of humility when He told the story of the Good
Samaritan. Thieves assault and rob a man leaving him
on the side of the road. A priest traveling the road sees
the injured man and passes by. Then a man who serves
in the synagogue, a Levite, does the same thing. They
passed up an opportunity to serve because of their pride.
They only thought of themselves. Another man came
by, a Samaritan. The Samaritans were the enemies of
the Israelites. (Imagine a Nazi soldier helping an Allied
soldier during World War II.) The Samaritan was moved
with compassion. In humility he stopped, bandaged his
wounds, transported him to an inn, paid for lodging and
food, and left extra money behind for his medical care.
The Samaritan personifies humility.

We often miss opportunities to serve Jesus because
of our pride. We consider ourselves too important.
Sometimes, we care too much about our social position

or lifestyle to serve the poor or travel to a foreign country without indoor plumbing. When we see someone in need and have the ability to help, but walk on by because of our pride, we are missing the Lord.

I know a pastor who leads a large church, and you can often see him picking up litter in the parking lot, leaning underneath a leaky pipe with his tools, or mopping up a mess in a restroom. He lives in complete humility, not too proud to stoop.

A PRAYER FOR HELP

Beloved Jesus, I want to be like You. I want to have the same attitude as You. An attitude of a servant. Help me love and serve others like You did when You washed the disciples feet. In Your precious name, I pray. Amen.

To be faithful means to finish, no matter the cost. A faithful person follows instructions and doesn't quit or give up when difficulties flare up. A faithful person can be trusted and depended upon. Faithful people are consistently trustworthy. They are loyal to people, promises, and duties.

Jesus taught a profound axiom.

> *"Whoever can be trusted with very little can also be trusted with much, and whoever is dishonest with very little will also be dishonest with much. So if you have not been trustworthy in handling worldly wealth, who will trust you with true riches? And if you have not been trustworthy with someone else's property, who will give you property of your own?"*
> *—Luke 16:10-12*

This is the rule of faithfulness. If we desire greater things, we must be good stewards—managers—of what we have now. Jesus mentioned wealth and property in His teaching, but the rule applies to talents, gifts, personality, friendships, responsibilities, and more.

Jesus taught on this subject with another parable—the Parable of the Talents (Matthew 25:14-30). Of the three servants who were given assignments, two were faithful in their duties and tasks. The master rewarded each greatly and praised each with these words: "Well done, good and faithful servant; you have been faithful over a few things, I will make you ruler over many things. Enter into the joy of your lord" (Matthew 25:23).

My wife, June, demonstrates faithfulness in so many ways. Several years ago, she desired to teach a Bible study in our neighborhood. She invited several ladies, however only one showed up at the first meeting. Then she showed up again the next week. My wife taught and discipled this woman for four years. She could've given up or been discouraged. She could've believed the lie that God had not called her to lead this study. Instead, she was faithful. And the Lord honored her faithfulness with a ministry of teaching at conferences, retreats, and women's Bible studies. She now ministers to hundreds because she was faithful to minister to one.

Ben was excited when given the opportunity to lead worship for a home Bible study group. He had played the guitar for a few years, but wasn't very accomplished—especially at singing and playing at the same time. He remained persistent and faithful to practice, learn new songs, and lead the group, and God blessed him. Over a period of time, Ben's talents grew and his opportunities increased. He now leads Sunday morning worship at his church.

If we will simply be faithful to use our gifts, talents, abilities, time, resources, and personality as God directs us, He will open up more and larger opportunities. As you are faithful with the new opportunities, you will discover the ministry God has for you.

A PRAYER FOR HELP

Holy Father, thank You for the opportunities You've given me. I'm sorry that I didn't work as hard as I could. Help me to be faithful, give me endurance, close my ears to my critics, and allow me to glorify You. In Jesus' name, Amen.

BE FOCUSED

To be focused means giving your attention to one thing, concentrating on a single goal, being single-minded. To be focused in ministry, we must remain focused on what the Lord Jesus has given us to do—our mission and ministry.

Race horses often wear blinders so they can only see the goal ahead, not their surroundings. The blinders keep them focused on the finish line they have been trained to reach. An old adage reminds, "Keep the main thing the main thing." An old proverb warns, "He who is busy with two things drowns. He who paddles two canoes sinks." Focus. Focus. Focus.

The Bible is full of examples of focus...and the lack of it.

Peter sank when he was walking on water because he took his focus off of Jesus.

When Jesus came into the house of Martha and Mary, Martha was distracted about many things, but Mary was focused on one thing—worshiping Jesus. (Mark 10:40-41).

Paul was keeping his focus when he declared, "Not that I have already attained, or am already perfected; but I press on, that I may lay hold of that for which Christ Jesus has also laid hold of me. Brethren, I do not count myself to have apprehended; but one thing I do, forgetting those things which are behind and reaching forward to those things which are ahead, I press toward the goal for the prize of the upward call of God in Christ Jesus" (Philippians 3:12-14).

Jesus, with great focus, moved toward his arrest, trial, death, burial, and resurrection. "Now it came to pass, when the time had come for Him to be received up, that He steadfastly set His face to go to Jerusalem" (Luke 9:58).

David, who was often distracted, sang about his "one thing." "One thing I ask of the Lord, this is what I seek: that I may dwell in the house of the Lord all the days of my life, to gaze upon the beauty of the Lord and to seek him in his temple" (Psalm 27:4).

The Holy Spirit sent Philip to a desert place and a ministry. He shared the Gospel with the Ethiopian. His focused mission was complete and the Lord mysteriously made him disappear (Acts 8:26-40). Philip remained focused on evangelism throughout his life (Acts 20).

While on vacation in Colorado, we visited Pikes Peak. The annual Pikes Peak marathon, one of the most difficult in the United States, was coming to a close. My family and I watched the final runners struggle to cross the finish line. Some were barely able to put one foot in front of the other, yet, they kept their minds and eyes focused on the finish line. Keeping their focus, they reached their goal.

A PRAYER FOR HELP

Lord Jesus, thank You for always remaining focused on Your mission—redeeming Your creation. Thank You for turning Your focus toward me. Help me to set my face toward the goals You have for me. In Your almighty name, Amen.

Being filled means allowing our hearts to be full of the Holy Spirit's presence. It also means being empowered by the Holy Spirit. When we are filled, we trust and depend upon His strength instead of our own abilities. We must also allow our ears to be filled with the voice of the Holy Spirit so we can follow His instructions.

Paul offers a rich analogy. "Do not get drunk on wine, which leads to debauchery. Instead, be filled with the Spirit" (Ephesians 5:18). Being filled can be compared to being "under the influence" of the Holy Spirit. Excessive drinking impairs vision, judgment, the body's motor functions, and speech. In contrast, being filled with the Spirit gives us greater focus, opens access to greater wisdom and knowledge, and can help us accomplish seemingly impossible tasks.

Jesus did not begin His earthly ministry until the Holy Spirit came upon Him (Matthew 3:16, 17).

Jesus' followers, about 120 of them, waited in a room in Jerusalem until God poured out the Holy Spirit on the day of Pentecost. This outpouring marks the beginning of the Church.

The Spirit-filled life is a surrendered life. If Jesus did not begin His earthly ministry until the Holy Spirit came upon Him and the Church did not begin until the Holy Spirit was poured out upon them, how much more do you and I need to be filled with the Holy Spirit.

Jesus did not work any miracles or perform any supernatural acts, until the Spirit descended upon Him. After His ascension, His disciples could not perform any miracles until the Holy Spirit came. Paul was filled with the Holy Spirit three days after his salvation in Damascus.

If you were to take a large, empty, pickle jar and fill it with small pebbles, you could get a lot of pebbles inside. If there was no room for any more pebbles you would consider the jar filled. But if took the pickle jar "full" of pebbles and began to pour in handfuls of sand, you would see the sand settle around the pebbles. When you could pour no more sand into the jar, you might then consider it full. However, if you began to slowly pour water into the jar "full" of pebbles and sand, you would see the water fill up every remaining molecule of space. In a few minutes, the water would overflow the jar.

The Spirit-filled life is like being a jar: until we are filled to overflowing with the Holy Spirit, we are not fully filled. The Holy Spirit needs to seep into and permeate every part of our lives until we overflow with Him.

A PRAYER FOR HELP

Holy Spirit, fill me up. Fill me to overflowing so that I may be fully used for Your will. Let me not push away Your filling. Fill my ears with Your voice and my soul with Your presence. In Jesus' name, Amen

APPENDIX

THE GIFTS OF THE SPIRIT

*"But the manifestation of the Spirit is given to
each one for the profit of all..."*
1 Corinthians 12:7 NKJV

Word of wisdom is a supernatural ability given for direction and guidance. Wisdom is the proper application of fact or knowledge. It is God's answer to our dilemma. (1 Corinthians 12:8; Acts 6:3; 2 Chronicles 20:15; John 4:16; 1 Kings 3:16-20)

Word of knowledge is the supernatural revelation of information we could not know naturally. It is knowledge concerning specific situations, events, or persons. (1 Corinthians 12:8; John 4:51; John 4:16; 2 Kings 5:25; 1 Samuel 10:22)

Faith, the gift, goes beyond saving faith and faith which is the fruit of the Spirit. It is a supernatural ability given to believe God for unique circumstances, to have extraordinary confidence in the will and purpose of God.

(1 Corinthians 12:9; 1 Corinthians 13:2; Acts 6:8; Acts 3:1-16; 1 Kings 18:38; 1 Kings 17:1-7)

Gifts of healings is a supernatural ability given by God to heal the sick that need their health restored, either spiritually, mentally, or physically. (1 Corinthians 12:9; Mark 16:17, 18; Acts 4:30-32; Acts 8:5-8; Mark 8:22-28; John 9:6, 7; Matthew 4:23-25 Isaiah 53:1-5; Exodus 15:26)

Working of miracles is a supernatural ability given to perform something that is humanly impossible, and supersedes the natural laws of God's universe. (1 Corinthians 12:9; Acts 2:22; Mark 16:17, 18; Acts 8:6, 7; Acts 19:11, 12; Acts 4:16)

Prophecy is a supernatural ability given to speak forth the words from God for edification, exhortation, and comfort which means to build up, to stir up, and to cheer up. (1 Corinthians 12:10; Acts 2:17; Acts 21:9; 1 Timothy 1:18; 1 Timothy 4:14; 1 Corinthians 14:3, 4; Romans 12:6)

Discerning of spirits is a supernatural ability given to know the source of activity; whether or not the source is from God's Holy Spirit, an evil spirit, or the human spirit.

(1 Corinthians 12:10; Matthew 9:27-34; Acts 16:16-18; Acts 8:8-23)

Tongues is a supernatural ability given for prayer and praise to God in a language that is unknown to the one who is speaking. (1 Corinthians 12:10; 1 Corinthians 13:1; 1 Corinthians 14:1-40; Mark 16:17; Acts 2:4; Acts 10:44-48; Acts 19:1-7)

Interpretation of tongues is a supernatural ability to make known what is spoken in tongues. It is an *interpretation* and not a *translation*. It is a companion gift to the gift of tongues. (1 Corinthians 12:10; 1 Corinthians 14:1-40)

Helps is a special ability to see specific needs and to meet them quietly and diligently without the need for public recognition. (1 Corinthians 12:28; Romans 16: 1, 2; Acts 9:36-39)

Exhortation is the special ability to encourage and urge others to put into action the things one should be doing. (Romans 12:8; Titus 1:9; 2 Timothy 4:2; 1 Thessalonians 2:3-7)

Giving is the special ability given by the Holy Spirit to enable one to share their finances, and/or their material resources with liberality and cheerfulness. (Romans 12:8.)

Teaching is the special ability to give clarity to the word of God and present it in a way that gives practical application of it. (1 Corinthians 12:28; Acts 18:24-28; 2 Timothy 3:14-17; 1 Timothy 3:2)

Celibacy is a special ability to certain members of the body of Christ to remain single and enjoy it; to be unmarried and not suffer undue sexual temptations. (1 Corinthians 7:7-8; Matthew 19:10-12)

Intercession is a special ability to certain members of the body of Christ to pray for extended periods of time on a regular basis and see frequent and specific answers to their prayers to the degree much greater than that which is expected of the average Christian. (Romans 8:26; James 5: 14-16; 1 John 2:1; Isaiah 53:12; Hebrews 7:25; Ezekiel 22:30)

Martyrdom is that special ability to certain members of the body of Christ to undergo suffering for their faith even to the point of death, while consistently displaying a joyous and victorious attitude which brings glory to God. (1 Corinthians 13:3; Acts 7:54-60)

Leadership is the special ability given by the Holy Spirit to lead, direct, oversee, and govern others. (Romans 12:8; Hebrews 13:17; Luke 9:51)

Administration is the special ability to organize people, events, or circumstances as needed. (1 Corinthians 12:28; Acts 6:1-7)

Mercy is the special ability to reach out to others in compassion and tenderness and is exercised cheerfully in deeds that reflect the love of Jesus Christ. (Romans 12:8; Luke 10:37; Hebrews 4:16; Colossians 3:12; Mark 9:41)

Hospitality is the special ability to welcome visitors and to make them comfortable. (1 Timothy 3:2; Acts 16:15; Acts 20:20; Philemon 2)

Serving is the special ability to see needs and to quietly respond to them by using the available resources. (Romans 12:7; Ephesians 4:12; Acts 6:1-7)

Apostleship is the special ability to teach God's word and establish churches. Today we consider missionaries to be fulfilling this office. (Ephesians 4:11-14; Acts 8:5-6; Acts 13:1-4)

Prophet is one who has the special ability to speak forth a divine message that can at times include a future event. This could also be to give warning of difficulties that lie ahead. (1 Corinthians 12:28; Ephesians 4:11-14; Romans 12:6; Luke 7:26; Acts 15:32)

Evangelist is one who has the special ability to preach the gospel and proclaiming Jesus Christ's death, forgiveness of sin and salvation through receiving Jesus Christ as Savior. (Ephesians 4:11-14; Acts 13:1-3; Acts 21:8)

Pastor/Teacher is the special ability to pastor or shepherd God's flock which includes guarding, feeding, and strengthening. (Ephesians 4:11-14; 1 Timothy 3:1-7; John 10:1-18; 1 Peter 5:1-3)